PRE-TRAINEESHIP
MATHS & LITERACY FOR
RETAIL

graduated exercises and practice exam

Andrew Spencer

A+ National Pre-traineeship Maths & Literacy for Retail
1st Edition
Andrew Spencer

Associate publishing editor: Jana Raus
Project editor: Jana Raus
Senior designer: Vonda Pestana
Text design: Vonda Pestana
Cover design: Ami-Louise Sharpe
Cover image: Photolibrary
Photo research: Libby Henry
Production controller: Alex Ross
Reprint: Jess Lovell
Typeset by Knowledgeworks Global Limited

Any URLs contained in this publication were checked for currency during the production process. Note, however, that the publisher cannot vouch for the ongoing currency of URLs.

Acknowledgements

We would like to thank the following for permission to reproduce copyright material:

Jupiterimages Corporation: p. 33; Photolibrary: p.21; Shutterstock/SasPartout: p. 19.

Every effort has been made to trace and acknowledge copyright. However, if any infringement has occurred the publishers tender their apologies and invite the copyright holders to contact them.

For product information and technology assistance,
in Australia call **1300 790 853**;
in New Zealand call **0800 449 725**

For permission to use material from this text or product, please email **aust.permissions@cengage.com**

ISBN 978 0 17 046279 2

Cengage Learning Australia
Level 7, 80 Dorcas Street
South Melbourne, Victoria Australia 3205

Cengage Learning New Zealand
Unit 4B Rosedale Office Park
331 Rosedale Road, Albany, North Shore 0632, NZ

For learning solutions, visit **cengage.com.au**

Printed in Australia by Ligare Pty Ltd
1 2 3 4 5 6 7 25 24 23 22 21

A+ National

PRE-TRAINEESHIP

Maths & Literacy for Retail

Contents

Introduction

has always been important to understand, from a teacher's perspective, the nature of mathematical skills students need for their future, rather than teaching them textbook mathematics. This has been a guiding principle behind the development of the content in this workbook. To teach maths that is *relevant* to students seeking apprenticeships is the best that we can do, to give students an education in the field they would like to work in.

The content in this resource is aimed at the level that is needed for a student to have the best possibility of improving their mathematical and literacy skills specifically for trades. Students can use this workbook to prepare for an apprenticeship entry assessment, or to even assist with basic numeracy and literacy at the VET/TAFE level. Coupled with the NelsonNet website, https://www.nelsonnet.con.au/free-resources, these resources have the potential to improve students' understanding of basic mathematical concepts that can be applied to trades. These resources have been trialled, and they work.

Commonly used trade terms are introduced so that students have a basic understanding of terminology they will encounter in the workplace environment. Students who can complete this workbook and reach an 80% or higher outcome in all topics will have achieved the goal of this resource. These students will go on to complete work experience, do a VET accredited course, or will be able to gain entry into VET/TAFE or an apprenticeship in the trade of their choice.

The content in this workbook is the first step to bridging the gap between what has been learned in previous years, and what needs to be remembered and re-learned for use in trades. Students will significantly benefit from the consolidation of the basic maths and literacy concepts.

Every school has students who want to work with their hands, and not all students want to go to university. The best students want to learn what they don't know, and if students want to learn, then this book has the potential to give them a good start in life.

This resource has been specifically tailored to prepare students for sitting apprenticeship or VET/TAFE admission tests, and for giving students the basic skills they will need for a career in trade. In many ways, it is a 'win-win situation', with students enjoying and studying relevant maths for trades and Registered Training Organisations (RTOs) receiving students that have improved basic maths and literacy skills.

All that is needed is patience, hard work, a positive attitude, a belief in yourself that you can do it and a desire to achieve. The rest is up to you.

About the author

Andrew Spencer has studied education both within Australia and overseas. He has a Bachelor of Education, as well as a Masters of Science in which he specialised in teacher education. Andrew has extensive experience in teaching secondary mathematics throughout New South Wales and South Australia for well over fifteen years. He has taught a range of subject areas, including Maths, English, Science, Classics, Physical Education and Technical Studies. His sense of the importance of practical mathematics has continued to develop with the range of subject areas he has taught in.

Acknowledgements

For Paula, Zach, Katelyn, Mum and Dad.

Many thanks to Mal Aubrey (GTA) and all training organisations for their input.

To the De La Salle Brothers for their selfless work with all students.

Thanks also to Dr. Pauline Carter for her unwavering support of all maths teachers.

This is for all students who value learning, who are willing to work hard and who have character … and are characters!

Unit 1: Spelling

Short-answer questions

Specific instructions to students

- This is an exercise to help you identify and to correct spelling errors.
- Read the activity below, then answer accordingly.

Read the following passage and identify and correct the spelling errors.

Alice and Darren go shopping at the local shopping centre. The shopping centre is very bussy as the retail outlats are having hugge sales. Over 300 shops are located there, and with late-night shoping, peope offen stay for a meal. Alice and Darren both head for the clothing shops first to chek out the different desiner labels. They both like the jeans on sale but they don't have enugh money to buy anythang. Then Darren sees some t-shirts that look awesome, and he has just enough to buy two. Alice wants to look at mobile phones, so they both head off to find the stoure.

They locate the mobile phone store in the midle of the shopping centre, and inside there are two staff members. Alice looks at the pre-paid phones while Darren looks at the range of mobile phone covars. Alice asks if she can see a top-of-the-range pre-paid phone. The staff mumber shows her the best one available, and explains that it comes free with their $99-per-month phone plan. By choosing this plan, she would get over $130 in credit each month but she would have to sighn up for 24 months. Alice thanks the staff member and walks over to Darren, who is now looking at the mobile phones on the other side of the shop. Darren is thinking of upgruding his mobile, but isn't sure if he can afford it as most of the newer mobiles cost him a fair bit. Alice and Darren deside to leave it for now and grab a bite to eat as they are both getting hungray.

The food court is really busy, but they manage to find an empty table to sit down at. They look up at the menus above the food stands and narrow their choices down to the following: chickan nugets with chips, chicken vinduloo, lasagnia, pork and vegetuble cury, beef vinduloo, chilli con carne or a hamburgar with chips. It is getting late so they hurriedly oarder and eat their meal before going to the music store. Alice and Darren both love musik and it isn't hard to spend money in the store. Both walk out with two CDs each. They were on specal, with a 20% discount. It is now almost 9.00 p.m. so they decide to head over to the bus stasion and catch a bus home.

Incorrect words:

_____

_____

_____

Correct words:

_____

_____

_____

9780170462792

Unit 2: Alphabetising

Put the following words into alphabetical order.

Sale	Stock take
Credit card	Pricing
Repayment	Mid-year sales
CD	Checkout
Coffee shop	Security
Ice cream	Trolley
Store manager	Audit

Answer:

_____

_____

_____

_____

_____

_____

_____

_____

_____

_____

_____

_____

_____

_____

Short-answer questions

Specific instructions to students

- This is an exercise to help you understand what you read.
- Read the following activity, then answer the questions that follow.

Read the following passage and answer the questions in sentence form.

The students had a day off school so they decided to go to the local shopping centre. David was the only one that had his licence so he was the designated driver. The other three students got into the car and they made their way to the shopping centre. When they got there they all piled out of the car and went to the food court. They were all hungry as no one had had breakfast, and it was already 10.00 a.m. Ian bought a chocolate thickshake for $2.80, Bruce bought a hotdog meal deal which included a drink for $4.95, Julie bought a donut and an ice cream for $3.95 and David had a piece of cheesecake for $3.95. They all sat down and ate before Ian and Bruce headed off to look at the bicycle shop. Ian had had his bike stolen two weeks earlier, so he was in the market for a new one.

David and Julie went into the jeans shop first to have a look at the newest jeans that had come in. Julie tried on a pair of jeans before buying them, but David didn't end up buying anything. After that, David and Julie headed to the surf shop where David bought a new pair of skates for $59.99.

They all met up again outside the cinema as they were keen to see a movie. It was Cheap Tuesday, so all the tickets only cost $10 for any movie. David, Ian and Bruce all bought a popcorn and drink deal that cost $9.90 each. Julie only wanted a drink and this cost her $3.50. They all walked to Cinema 3 where the movie was screening and sat in the back row. The start time for the movie was 2.00 p.m. and it finished at 3.55 p.m. After the movie they all went back to David's place and stayed there until 6.00 p.m. before heading home.

QUESTION 1

Who drove to the shopping centre and why?

Answer:

How much money did all four spend in total at the food court?

Answer:

_____

QUESTION 3
Why did Ian want to look in the bicycle shop?

Answer:

_____

QUESTION 4
How much did all four spend in total at the movies?

Answer:

_____

QUESTION 5
How long did the group spend at the shopping centre? State your answer in hours and minutes.

Answer:

_____

MATHEMATICS

Unit 4: General Mathematics

Short-answer questions

Specific instructions to students

- This unit will help you to improve your general mathematical skills.
- Read the following questions and answer all of them in the spaces provided.
- You may not use a calculator.
- You need to show all working.

QUESTION 1

What unit of measurement would you use to measure:

a the size of a person's waistline for fitting jeans?

Answer:

_____

b the temperature of an oven in a patisserie?

Answer:

_____

c the change given from a dollar coin?

Answer:

_____

d the weight of a jumper?

Answer:

_____

e the speed of a delivery truck?

Answer:

_____

f the height of a retail shop?

Answer:

_____

g the weight of a fridge?

Answer:

_____

QUESTION 2

Write an example of each of the following and give an instance where it may be found in the retail industry.

a Percentages

Answer:

_____

b Decimals

Answer:

_____

_____

c Fractions

Answer:

_____

_____

d Mixed numbers

Answer:

_____

_____

e Ratios

Answer:

_____

_____

f Angle

Answer:

_____

QUESTION 3

Convert the following units:

a 12 kg to g

Answer:

_____

b 4 tonnes to kilograms

Answer:

_____

9780170462792

c 120 cm to m

Answer:

d 1140 millitres to litres

Answer:

e 1650 g to kg

Answer:

f 1880 kilograms to tonnes

Answer:

g 13 m to cm

Answer:

h 4.5 litres to millitres

Answer:

QUESTION 4
Write the following in descending order:

0.4   0.04   4.1   40.0   400.00   4.0

Answer:

QUESTION 5
Write the decimal number that goes between the following:

a 0.2 and 0.4

Answer:

b 1.8 and 1.9

Answer:

c 12.4 and 12.6

Answer:

d 28.3 and 28.4

Answer:

e 101.5 and 101.7

Answer:

QUESTION 6
Round off the following numbers to two (2) decimal places:

a 12.346

Answer:

b 2.251

Answer:

c 123.897

Answer:

d 688.882

Answer:

e 1209.741

Answer:

QUESTION 7
Estimate the following by approximation:

a $1288 \times 19 =$

Answer:

b $201 \times 20 =$

Answer:

c $497 \times 12.2 =$

Answer:

d $1008 \times 10.3 =$

Answer:

e $399 \times 22 =$

Answer:

f $201 - 19 =$

Answer:

g $502 - 61 =$

Answer:

h 1003 − 49 =

Answer:

i 10 001 − 199 =

Answer:

j 99.99 − 39.8 =

Answer:

QUESTION 8
What do the following add up to?

a $4, $4.99 and $144.95

Answer:

b $8.75, $6.9 and $12.55

Answer:

c 65 mL, 18 mL + 209 mL

Answer:

d 21.3 g, 119.8 g + 884.6 g

Answer:

QUESTION 9
Subtract the following:

a 2338 from 7117

Answer:

b 1786 from 3112

Answer:

c 5979 from 8014

Answer:

d 11 989 from 26 221

Answer:

e 108 767 from 231 111

Answer:

QUESTION 10
Use division to solve the following:

a 2177 divided by 7

Answer:

b 4484 ÷ 4

Answer:

c 63.9 divided by 0.3

Answer:

d 121.63 ÷ 1.2

Answer:

e 466.88 ÷ 0.8

Answer:

The following information is provided for Question 11.

To solve using BODMAS, in order from left to right solve the Brackets first, then Of, then Division, then Multiplication, then Addition and lastly Subtraction. The following example has been done for your reference.

EXAMPLE:

Solve $(4 \times 7) \times 2 + 6 - 4$.

STEP 1

Solve the Brackets first: $(4 \times 7) = 28$

STEP 2

No Division so next solve Multiplication: $28 \times 2 = 56$

STEP 3

Addition is next: $56 + 6 = 62$

STEP 4

Subtraction is the last process: $62 - 4 = 58$

FINAL ANSWER:

58

9780170462792

QUESTION 11

Using BODMAS solve:

a $(6 \times 9) \times 5 + 7 - 2$

Answer:

_____

b $(9 \times 8) \times 4 + 6 - 1$

Answer:

_____

c $3 \times (5 \times 7) + 11 - 8$

Answer:

_____

d $6 + 9 - 5 \times (8 \times 3)$

Answer:

_____

e $9 - 7 + 6 \times 3 + (9 \times 6)$

Answer:

_____

f $(4 \times 3) - 6 + 9 \times 4 + (6 \times 7)$

Answer:

_____

g $(4 \times 9) - (3 \times 7) + 16 - 11 \times 2$

Answer:

_____

h $9 - 4 \times 6 + (6 \times 7) + (8 \times 9) - 23$

Answer:

_____

Unit 5: Basic Operations

Section A: Addition

Short-answer questions

Specific instructions to students

- This section will help you to improve your addition skills for basic operations.
- Read the questions below and answer all of them in the spaces provided.
- You may not use a calculator.
- You need to show all working.

QUESTION 1

A shopper buys 200 g of ham, 150 g of salami and 270 g of shaved turkey. How many grams is that in total?

Answer:

QUESTION 2

A launderer buys packets of washing powder in three different sizes: 1.5 kg, 2.5 kg and 15 kg. How many kilograms of washing powder has he purchased in total?

Answer:

QUESTION 3

A jewellery store stocks 327 rings, 368 bracelets and 723 various other pieces of fine jewellery. How many pieces does it stock in total?

Answer:

QUESTION 4

A delivery van is driven 352 km, 459 km, 872 km and 198 km over 4 consecutive weeks. How far has the van been driven in total?

Answer:

QUESTION 5

A furniture delivery van uses the following amounts of diesel over a month: 35.5 litres in week one, 42.9 litres in week two, 86.9 litres in week 3 and 66.2 litres in week four.

a How many litres were used in total?

Answer:

b If diesel costs $1.95 per litre, how much was spent on fuel for the month?

Answer:

QUESTION 6

A shopper buys a frying pan for $82.50, 4 dicing knives for $116.80 and a mixing bowl for $6.75, how much has been spent?

Answer:

QUESTION 7

A cook buys 10 kg of mince and divides it into three containers of 2.6 kg, 3.2 kg and 1.8 kg. How many kg have been used?

Answer:

9780170462792

QUESTION 8

A shopper buys a new steam cooker for $225.80, a chopping block for $26.99 and a set of knives for $88.50. How much has been spent in total?

Answer:

_____

QUESTION 9

A worker travels 36 km, 33 km, 37 km and 44 km over four weeks to get to and from the shopping centre where she works. How far has she travelled in total?

Answer:

_____

QUESTION 10

175 g, 180 g and 100 g of bacon are purchased to make different meals in a coffee shop. How much bacon was purchased in total?

Answer:

_____

Section B: Subtraction

Short-answer questions

Specific instructions to students

- This section will help you to improve your subtraction skills for basic operations.
- Read the following questions and answer all of them in the spaces provided.
- You may not use a calculator.
- You need to show all working.

QUESTION 1

A shopper buys a 10 litre can of virgin olive cooking oil. He uses 1.2 litres for cooking on one night, 1.7 litres on the next night and 1.1 litres on the third night.

a How much oil is used in total?

Answer:

_____

b How much oil is left in the can?

Answer:

_____

QUESTION 2

If one person uses 151 g of flour to make a cake and another person uses 169 g to make another, how much more flour has the first person used than the second?

Answer:

_____

QUESTION 3

A worker earns $650 per week. He spends $24.80 on food and $94.70 on petrol. How much is left?

Answer:

_____

QUESTION 4

A surf shop sells 39 bracelets from a box that contains 200 bracelets. How many are left?

Answer:

_____

QUESTION 5

The total bill for skate gear comes to $154.65. The manager takes off a discount of $15. How much does the bill now total?

Answer:

_____

QUESTION 6

Over the course of a year, a store manager drives 11 297 km. Of this, 1835 km was for her personal use, while the rest was for work. How far did she drive for work-related purposes?

Answer:

_____

QUESTION 7

A delivery truck uses the following amounts of diesel over 3 months:

Month 1 – 225 litres

Month 2 – 313 litres

Month 3 – 296 litres

a How much diesel is used?

Answer:

_____

b 1000 litres is budgeted for the 3 months. How much is left?

Answer:

_____

QUESTION 8

During one month, a worker budgets to spend $34 on bus tickets. When he goes to purchase the tickets in bulk, he hands over a $100 note. How much change will he get?

Answer:

_____

QUESTION 9

The yearly rental on a small shop comes to $24 231. The parents of a young owner help by putting $3,500 into the business to assist with the rent. How much more needs to be paid?

Answer:

_____

QUESTION 10

A barista uses the following amounts of milk in three cups of hot beverages: 57 mL, 69 mL and 53 mL. If there were 2 litres of milk to begin with, how much would be left?

Answer:

_____

Section C: Multiplication

Short-answer questions

Specific instructions to students

- This section will help you to improve your multiplication skills for basic operations.
- Read the following questions and answer all of them in the spaces provided.
- You may not use a calculator.
- You need to show all working.

QUESTION 1

If a dry-cleaning van travels at 60 km/h, how far will it travel in 6 hours?

Answer:

_____

QUESTION 2

If a clothing delivery van travels at 80 km/h, how far will it travel in 8 hours?

Answer:

_____

QUESTION 3

A courier uses 8 litres of fuel to get to and from work each day. How much fuel is used if the same trip is completed 26 times?

Answer:

_____

QUESTION 4

A jeweller has a sale on with the following items discounted: a ring that has half a carat of diamonds set in 18 ct gold for $849, a diamond-set pendant with a 9 ct gold chain for $145 and gold hoop earrings for $199. If a shopper buys two of each item, how much do they spend in total?

Answer:

_____

QUESTION 5

At a food barn, a shopper buys 4 green capsicums for 99 cents each, 2 red onions for 45 cents each and 2 lettuces for $1.39 each. What is the total cost?

Answer:

QUESTION 6

A shopper purchases 16 bread rolls. If one bread roll costs 45 cents, how much do the 16 cost in total?

Answer:

QUESTION 7

A storeman's car uses 12 litres of LPG for every 100 km driven. How much LPG would be used for 400 km?

Answer:

QUESTION 8

A retail assistant earns $285 per month. If she earns the same amount each month, how much would she earn over a year?

Answer:

QUESTION 9

If 11 fridges are purchased each day in a large retail chain store, how many would be purchased wide over a 30-day month?

Answer:

QUESTION 10

If a car travels at 110 km/h for 5 hours, how far has it travelled in total?

Answer:

Section D: Division

Short-answer questions

Specific instructions to students

- This section will help you to improve your division skills for basic operations.
- Read the following questions and answer all of them in the spaces provided.
- You may not use a calculator.
- You need to show all working.

QUESTION 1

In a crowded store, 120 units of one item need to be stocked on 4 shelves. How many items will fit on each shelf?

Answer:

QUESTION 2

A store manager earns $785 for working a 5-day week. How much does she earn per day?

Answer:

QUESTION 3

A shop assistant in an electronics store needs to put out 24 packets of earphones onto 3 shelves. How many earphones will fit on each shelf?

Answer:

QUESTION 4

A whitegoods delivery van covers 780 km in a 5-day week. How many km per day has been travelled on average?

Answer:

QUESTION 5

A shipment of 30 computer workstations weighs 750 kilograms. How much does each computer workstation weigh?

Answer:

QUESTION 6

An interstate semi-trailer travels 1825 km over a 7-day haul delivering clothing to retail outlets. Approximately how many km are covered, on average, each day?

Answer:

QUESTION 7

At a yearly stock take, a storeperson counts 720 of the same toys. There are 12 toys in each box.

a How many boxes are there?

Answer:

_____

b Are any toys left over?

Answer:

_____

QUESTION 8

The manager of a children's store orders 480 wrestling figures. When they arrive, the manager discovers that there are 6 wrestling figures in each box. How many boxes are there?

Answer:

_____

QUESTION 9

A furniture van carries 644 chairs to deliver to stores. The chairs are packed together in lots of 4. How many lots of chairs are there?

Answer:

_____

QUESTION 10

Some hardware needs to be transported from a warehouse to a computer shop. The manager of the computer shop finds that 240 modems were delivered. If there are 3 modems in each lot, how many lots will there be?

Answer:

_____

9780170462792

Unit 6: Decimals

Section A: Addition

QUESTION 1

A shopper buys a new mobile with a 24-month plan for $89.99, a new shirt for $36.50 and a DVD for $19.95. How much will the shopper pay in total?

Answer:

QUESTION 2

A family buys the following from a pet store: a puppy for $289.95, a kennel for $139.95 and pet food for $24.55. How much do the purchases come to in total?

Answer:

QUESTION 3

A cup holds 200 mL. If 30 mL of milk is added, as well as 20 mL of froth, what is the total?

Answer:

QUESTION 4

A curtain rod for a window measures 160.50 cm long and another is 80.5 cm. What is the total length of both?

Answer:

QUESTION 5

A shopper buys the following food: 5 kg of spaghetti for $8.99, a bottle of pasta sauce for $3.50 and 2 kg of mince for $12.50. What is the total cost?

Answer:

QUESTION 6

If a food delivery truck driver travels 65.8 km, 36.5 km, 22.7 km and 89.9 km, how far has been travelled in total?

Answer:

QUESTION 7

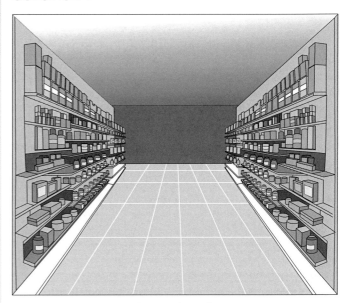

What is the total length of a shelf that measures 127.8 cm long that also has two attachment ends on it that each measure 10.5 cm?

Answer:

QUESTION 8

A bookcase has shelves that measure 35 cm, 32 cm, 38 cm and 42 cm in height. How tall is the bookcase?

Answer:

QUESTION 9

Three lay-by orders are being collected. The first order is worth $45.80, the second comes to $130.65 and the third is $116.45. How much is the total for all three?

Answer:

QUESTION 10

A shopper orders some lunch which includes soup for $4.50, a main meal of chicken with salad for $8.50 and dessert that costs $5.50. What does the total bill come to?

Answer:

Section B: Subtraction

Short-answer questions

Specific instructions to students

- This section will help you to improve your subtraction skills when working with decimals.
- Read the following questions and answer all of them in the spaces provided.
- You may not use a calculator.
- You need to show all working.

QUESTION 1

A barista pours 250 mL from a 2-litre bottle of milk to make some hot beverages. How much milk is left in the bottle?

Answer:

QUESTION 2

A sandwich-hand trims 2.5 cm of fat from a piece of bacon that is 31.4 cm long. How much bacon is left?

Answer:

QUESTION 3

A diner orders a meal that costs $8.20. She then receives a discount of $1.50.

a How much does the final bill come to?

Answer:

---

b How much change will she receive from $10.00?

Answer:

QUESTION 4

A shop assistant works 38 hours and earns $245.60. $29 is spent on petrol and $15 on a mobile phone recharge card. How much is left?

Answer:

QUESTION 5

A group of 4 people each put in $10 for food and drinks. If the bill comes to $28.90, how much change will they receive?

Answer:

QUESTION 6

A group of 3 friends go to the cinema. The cost of the tickets totals $41.50 and the total cost of popcorn and drinks comes to $26.50. If they have a total of $100.00, how much change will they have left?

Answer:

QUESTION 7

At a computer store, a shopper purchases 3 computer games that cost a total of $32.50. How much change will he receive from $50.00?

Answer:

QUESTION 8

A P-plate driver buys 4 litres of engine oil. However, his car is slowly leaking oil, and after 3 months the car uses up 285 mL, 160 mL and 1300 mL of oil for each month respectively.

a How much oil is used?

Answer:

b How much is left?

Answer:

QUESTION 9

A bill for lunch includes $23.50 for 2 meals, $7.50 for a desert and $14.45 for 3 coffees.

a What is the total cost?

Answer:

b If the bill is paid with a $50 note, how much change is given?

Answer:

QUESTION 10

A set of knives are purchased for a café at a cost of $80.50. If it is paid for with two $50 notes, how much change will be given?

Answer:

Section C: Multiplication

Short-answer questions

Specific instructions to students

- This section will help you to improve your multiplication skills when working with decimals.
- Read the following questions and answer all of them in the spaces provided.
- You may not use a calculator.
- You need to show all working.

QUESTION 1

A shopper goes to a sale where CDs are sold for $9.95. The shopper buys 6 CDs.

a What is the total cost?

Answer:

b How much change will the shopper receive from $70.00?

Answer:

QUESTION 2

A person buys 16 bottles of virgin olive oil. Each bottle costs $5.50.

a What is the total cost for the 16 bottles?

Answer:

b How much change will be received from a $100 note?

Answer:

QUESTION 3

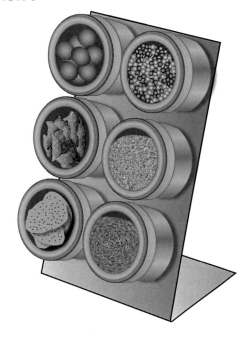

A consumer purchases 6 spice containers that cost $6.50 each and 4 bottles of pasta sauce at $3.95 per bottle.

a What is the total cost?

Answer:

_____

b How much change will the consumer receive from $55.00?

Answer:

_____

QUESTION 4

A group of 6 people dine at a restaurant that charges $16.50 per person for a banquet meal.

a How much is the total food bill?

Answer:

_____

b The diners tip the waiter $15.00. What does the total bill come to?

Answer:

_____

c How much change will they receive from $120.00?

Answer:

_____

QUESTION 5

Several supermarket workers go out for happy hour at the local pub. They have 9 cocktail drinks in total at a cost of $4.50 each.

a What is the total cost?

Answer:

_____

b How much change will they get from $50.00?

Answer:

_____

QUESTION 6

An entrée consists of 3 steamed dim sims. Each dim sim costs $2.20.

a How much does the entrée cost in total?

Answer:

_____

b How much change will the diners get from $10.00?

Answer:

_____

QUESTION 7

A canteen buys 120 pastries for $1.85 each. How much was spent in total?

Answer:

_____

QUESTION 8

A buyer places an order for 50 dozen oysters at $5.50 per dozen for a hotel.

a How much does the buyer pay in total?

Answer:

_____

b How much change will be needed from $300.00?

Answer:

_____

QUESTION 9

An event organiser orders 34 dinner rolls for a party.

a If each one costs $0.15, what is the outlay?

Answer:

_____

b How much change will she receive from $8.00?

Answer:

_____

QUESTION 10

A floor manager earns $180.65 per day. How much does he earn for 5 days?

Answer:

_____

9780170462792

Section D: Division

QUESTION 1

A supermarket shopper purchases 12 eggs for a total of $3.60. How much does each individual egg cost?

Answer:

_____

QUESTION 2

A store manager earns $990.50 for 5 days of work. How much does this work out to per day?

Answer:

_____

QUESTION 3

A restaurant bill totals $455.70 for 8 people. How much does each person pay if they split the bill evenly?

Answer:

_____

QUESTION 4

A food order at a bistro comes to $440.85 for 12 people. How much does each person pay if the bill is divided equally?

Answer:

_____

QUESTION 5

A surf shop serves 642 customers over 3 days during their summer sale. How many customers are served, on average, per day?

Answer:

_____

QUESTION 6

A store assistant who works at chemist and delivers prescriptions travels 889.9 km over 12 days. How far has been travelled, on average, each day?

Answer:

_____

QUESTION 7

A lunch wagon uses 11 litres of diesel to travel 257.3 km. How far does the wagon travel per litre?

Answer:

_____

QUESTION 8

A bag of flour weighing 2.5 kg is bought to be used in a recipe for 14 apple pies. How many grams of flour are needed per pie?

Answer:

_____

QUESTION 9

A group of 3 students walk into a restaurant and order some coffee and muffins. The bill comes to $33.99. How much is the cost per person, if the bill is divided equally?

Answer:

_____

QUESTION 10

A group of 5 people go to a deli. Each person in the group orders a chicken wrap, and the total comes to $31.60. How much does each person pay?

Answer:

_____

Unit 7: Fractions

Section A: Addition

QUESTION 1

$\frac{1}{2} + \frac{4}{5} = ?$

Answer:

_____

QUESTION 2

$1\frac{2}{3} + 1\frac{1}{2} = ?$

Answer:

_____

QUESTION 3

A carpet warehouse has 2 rolls of carpet. $\frac{1}{4}$ of a roll of Berber is left on one roll and $\frac{1}{3}$ of a roll of Berber is left on the other. How much Berber is there in total? Express your answer as a fraction.

Answer:

_____

QUESTION 4

An electronics store dedicates $\frac{1}{3}$ of the store to audio-visual and $\frac{2}{5}$ of the same store to mobile phone displays. How much as a fraction, of the store, has been taken up?

Answer:

_____

QUESTION 5

An ice cream shop uses $\frac{1}{3}$ of the counter for displaying advertising and $\frac{2}{4}$ of the counter for serving. How much of the counter, as a fraction, has been used?

Answer:

_____

Section B: Subtraction

QUESTION 1

$\frac{2}{3} - \frac{1}{4} = ?$

Answer:

_____

QUESTION 2

$2\frac{2}{3} - 1\frac{1}{4} = ?$

Answer:

_____

QUESTION 3

A shop assistant has a shelf that is $\frac{3}{4}$ full of toys. If she removes $\frac{1}{3}$ of the toys from the shelf, how much room is left? Express your answer as a fraction.

Answer:

QUESTION 4

A newsagency has a shelf that is $\frac{2}{4}$ full of lifestyle magazines. If $\frac{1}{3}$ of the magazines are removed from the shelf, as they are out of date, how much of the shelf is left? Express your answer as a fraction.

Answer:

QUESTION 5

A shop assistant working in a café has $2\frac{1}{4}$ cartons of milk on Monday to serve customers. A further $1\frac{1}{3}$ cartons of milk are used over Tuesday and Wednesday. How much milk is left? Express your answer as a fraction.

Answer:

Section C: Multiplication

Short-answer questions

Specific instructions to students

- This section is designed to help you to improve your multiplication skills when working with fractions.
- Read the following questions and answer all of them in the spaces provided.
- You may not use a calculator.
- You need to show all working.

QUESTION 1

$\frac{2}{4} \times \frac{2}{3} = ?$

Answer:

QUESTION 2

$2\frac{2}{3} \times 1\frac{1}{2} = ?$

Answer:

QUESTION 3

A delicatessen has 5 containers of lollies that are each $\frac{1}{4}$ full. If all of the lollies are combined, how many containers will they fill?

Answer:

QUESTION 4

A carpet shop has 3 rolls of carpet. Each has $\frac{1}{3}$ left on them. How much carpet is left in total? Express your answer as a fraction.

Answer:

QUESTION 5

A 24-hour shop stocks their fridges with soft drinks. If there are 4 shelves and they are all $\frac{1}{3}$ empty, how much shelf space, as a fraction, is left in the fridges?

Answer:

Section D: Division

Short-answer questions

Specific instructions to students

- This section is designed to help you to improve your division skills when working with fractions.
- Read the following questions and answer all of them in the spaces provided.
- You may not use a calculator.
- You need to show all working.

QUESTION 1

$\frac{2}{3} \div \frac{1}{4} = ?$

Answer:

QUESTION 2

$2\frac{3}{4} \div 1\frac{1}{3} = ?$

Answer:

QUESTION 3

A store manager has a length of bunting that measures $26\frac{1}{2}$ cm. It needs to be divided into $2\frac{1}{2}$ equal lengths. How long will each piece be?

Answer:

QUESTION 4

A shop assistant has $1\frac{2}{3}$ cans of ice cream. They need to be evenly divided into 3 separate containers. How much, as a fraction, will be put into each container?

Answer:

QUESTION 5

A juice bar has $2\frac{1}{2}$ bottles of tropical juice that needs to be evenly poured into 2 cups. How much, as a fraction, is used in each cup?

Answer:

Unit 8: Percentages

Short-answer questions

Specific instructions to students

- In this unit, you will be able to practice and improve your skills in working out percentages.
- Read the following questions and answer all of them in the spaces provided.
- You may not use a calculator.
- You need to show all working.

> **10% rule: Move the decimal one place to the left to get 10%.**

EXAMPLE

10% of $45.00 would be $4.50

QUESTION 1

A shopper buys a pair of jeans at a department store. The bill comes to $220.00 but then sees that there is a 10% off sale.

a How much is the discount worth?

Answer:

_____

b What does the final price of the jeans come to?

Answer:

_____

QUESTION 2

An assistant in a hardware store makes a sale that adds up to $249.00. However, there is a 10% discount sale on.

a How much is the discount worth?

Answer:

_____

b What does the sale total after the discount is taken off?

Answer:

_____

QUESTION 3

An air-conditioning company sells a 2 hp air conditioner for $698.50. The buyer is then given a 10% discount.

a How much is the discount worth?

Answer:

_____

b How much will the air conditioner cost after taking off the discount?

Answer:

_____

QUESTION 4

A store manager prices 2-litre bottles of cordial at $2.80 each. He then gives a 5% price reduction to help sell the bottles quickly.

a How much is the reduction worth?

Answer:

_____

b What is the final price of each cordial bottle? (Hint: find 10%, halve it to find 5%, then subtract it from $2.80.)

Answer:

_____

QUESTION 5

A student buys 3 roller storage bins for $20, a jacket for $69 and a DVD box set of $89.

a How much does the bill come to in total?

Answer:

_____

b When the student goes to pay at the register, she discovers that there is a 10% discount that applies to all of her items. How much does the bill total after the discount?

Answer:

_____

QUESTION 6

The following items are purchased: a pair of shorts for $39.99, a lamp for $19.99, a new shirt for $19.50, a mobile phone for $99, a new set of weights for $189 and some gardening tools for $14.25.

a What is the total cost?

Answer:

_____

b What is the final cost after a 10% discount is given?

Answer:

_____

c How much change would be received from $400.00?

Answer:

QUESTION 7

A food store offers 20% off the price of chocolate products. The cost of 4 items comes to $59.80 before the discount.

a How much is the discount?

Answer:

---

b What is the price after the discount?

Answer:

---

c What change would be needed from $70.00?

Answer:

QUESTION 8

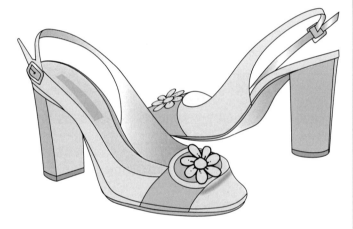

Leather shoes are discounted by 15% in a shoe store. The regular retail price of a certain pair is $85.60 each.

a How much is the discount worth?

Answer:

---

b What does the final sale price come to?

Answer:

---

c How much change would be received from $100.00?

Answer:

QUESTION 9

A shopper sees a packet of cashew nuts priced at $6.90. The shopper then discovers that the nut store has a 20% discount sale off all of its nuts.

a How much is the discount worth?

Answer:

---

b How much will the nuts cost after the discount?

Answer:

---

c How much change would be received from $10.00?

Answer:

QUESTION 10

A group of 5 people purchase tickets to the cinema at a cost of $70.00. The group also buys $43.60 worth of popcorn and drinks. One person has a voucher for 20% off the total price.

a How much will the discount be?

Answer:

---

b How much will the nuts cost after the discount?

Answer:

---

c How much change would be received from $100.00?

Answer:

9780170462792

Unit 9: Measurement Conversions

Short-answer questions

Specific instructions to students

- This unit is designed to help you to both improve your skills and to increase your speed in converting one measurement unit into another.
- Read the following questions and answer all of them in the spaces provided.
- You may not use a calculator.
- You need to show all working.

QUESTION 1

How many centimetres are there in 1 metre?

Answer:

QUESTION 2

How many millimetres are there in 1 metre?

Answer:

QUESTION 3

How many centimetres are there in 11 metres?

Answer:

QUESTION 4

How many cents are there in $3.75?

Answer:

QUESTION 5

How many cents are there in $10.83?

Answer:

QUESTION 6

How many centimetres are there in 1.25 metres of material?

Answer:

QUESTION 7

How many grams are in 1.2 kilograms of washing powder?

Answer:

QUESTION 8

How many millilitres are in 1.5 litres of soft drink?

Answer:

QUESTION 9

How many centimetres are in 1560 mm of pine?

Answer:

QUESTION 10

How many centimetres in 5850 millimetres of timber?

Answer:

Section A: Circumference

Short-answer questions

Specific instructions to students

- This section is designed to help you to both improve your skills and to increase your speed in measuring the circumference of a round object.
- Read the following questions and answer all of them in the spaces provided.
- You may not use a calculator.
- You will to show all working.

$C = \pi \times d$

where:

C = circumference

π = 3.14

d = diameter

EXAMPLE

Find the circumference of a plate with a diameter of 30 cm.

$C = \pi \times d$

Therefore, $C = 3.14 \times 30$

$= 94.2$ cm

QUESTION 1

Find the circumference of a display table with a diameter of 90 cm.

Answer:

_____

QUESTION 2

Calculate the circumference of a display board with a diameter of 15 cm.

Answer:

_____

QUESTION 3

Determine the circumference of a diamond ring with a diameter of 3 cm.

Answer:

_____

QUESTION 4

Find the circumference of a skim board with a diameter of 100 cm.

Answer:

_____

QUESTION 5

Determine the circumference of flood light with a diameter of 12 cm.

Answer:

_____

QUESTION 6

Calculate the circumference of a CD with a diameter of 22 cm.

Answer:

_____

QUESTION 7

Find the circumference of a Tupperware container with a diameter of 15.6 cm.

Answer:

_____

QUESTION 8

Determine the circumference of a kitchen exhaust fan with a diameter of 14.3 cm.

Answer:

_____

QUESTION 9

Find the circumference of a smoke alarm with a diameter of 12.9 cm.

Answer:

QUESTION 10

Calculate the circumference of an entrée plate with a diameter of 18.8 cm.

Answer:

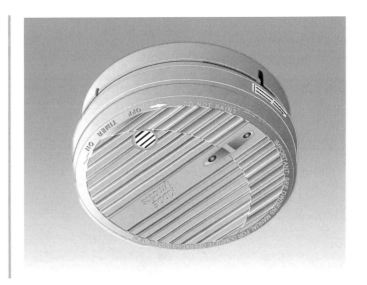

Section B: Diameter

Short-answer questions

Specific instructions to students

- This section is designed to help you to both improve your skills and to increase your speed in measuring the diameter of a round object.
- Read the following questions and answer all of them in the spaces provided.
- You may not use a calculator.
- You need to show all working.

Diameter (d) of a circle $= \dfrac{\text{circumference}}{\pi\,(3.14)}$

EXAMPLE

Find the diameter of a display table with a circumference of 800 cm.

$d = \dfrac{800}{3.14}$

$= 254.78$ cm

QUESTION 1

Find the diameter of a round mirror with a circumference of 120 cm.

Answer:

QUESTION 2

Determine the diameter of a wheel cover with a circumference of 600 cm.

Answer:

QUESTION 3

Calculate the diameter of a hotplate with a circumference of 50 cm.

Answer:

QUESTION 4

Find the diameter of a basin with a circumference of 200 cm.

Answer:

QUESTION 5

Calculate the diameter of a cut-off saw with a circumference of 430 cm.

Answer:

QUESTION 6

Find the diameter of a skylight with a circumference 140 cm.

Answer:

QUESTION 7

Determine the diameter of a glass feature window with a circumference of 135 cm.

Answer:

QUESTION 8

Calculate the diameter of a round table with a circumference of 280 cm.

Answer:

QUESTION 9

Find the diameter of a microwave dish with a circumference of 62 cm.

Answer:

QUESTION 10

Calculate the diameter of a deep fryer with a circumference of 68 cm.

Answer:

Section C: Area

> **Area = length × breadth and is given in square units.**
> $$= l \times b$$

QUESTION 1

The dimensions of a cooking tray sold in a homeware shop are 30 cm long by 12.8 cm wide. What is the total area of the tray?

Answer:

QUESTION 2

If the floor of a shop measures 20 m by 13 m, what is the total area?

Answer:

QUESTION 3

The dimensions of a display area is 2.85 m by 1.65 m. What is the total area?

Answer:

QUESTION 4

An area set aside to display toys measures 14.5 m by 12.8 m. What is the total area?

Answer:

QUESTION 5

What is the total area of a market stall that displays men's, women's and children's clothing that measures 13 m by 9 m?

Answer:

QUESTION 6

A hardware warehouse measures 335 m by 230 m. What is the total area?

Answer:

QUESTION 7

If a jewellery store's floor area is 12.06 m by 8.07 m, what is the total area?

Answer:

QUESTION 8

If a newsagent has a floor space of 6.53 m by 3.27 m, how much floor area is there?

Answer:

QUESTION 9

A whitegoods store allocates a display area for sinks, washing machines and bathroom accessories that is 38.2 m by 21.6 m. What is the total area?

Answer:

QUESTION 10

A fruit juice shop is 8.9 m long and 2.6 m wide. How much floor area is there?

Answer:

Section D: Volume of a Cube

> **Volume = length × width × height and is given in cubic units.**
>
> $= l \times w \times h$

QUESTION 1

How many cubic metres are there in an electrical retail outlet storage area 30 m long by 35 m wide by 4 m high?

Answer:

QUESTION 2

A cold storage delivery truck has the dimensions of 8 m in length by 3 m of width by 4 m of height. How many cubic metres are available?

Answer:

QUESTION 3

A refrigerated cold room measures 8 m × 3 m × 2 m. How many cubic metres are there?

Answer:

QUESTION 4

If a pasta shop uses a cooking tray for lasagne that measures 22 cm by 18 cm by 5 cm, how many cubic centimetres can it hold?

Answer:

QUESTION 5

A retail assistant uses a display case with the following dimensions: 60 cm by 15 cm by 10 cm. How many cubic centimetres can it hold?

Answer:

QUESTION 6

The back of a truck measures 2.8 m ×1.5 m × 2.2. What cubic area is available to use for storing goods?

Answer:

QUESTION 7

A storage box used by a retail store is 1m long, 60 cm wide and 75 cm tall. How many cubic centimetres are available for storage?

Answer:

QUESTION 8

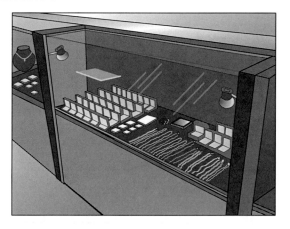

A jewellery display cabinet is 90 cm wide by 1 m long by 80 cm high. How much cubic area does it contain?

Answer:

QUESTION 9

A shelf in a major department store has the following dimensions: 0.75 m × 0.85 m × 2.6 m. What is its volume in cubic metres?

Answer:

QUESTION 10

An audio visual display cabinet is 2.8 m long by 1 m wide by 1.1 m high. How many cubic metres are available for displaying items?

Answer:

Section E: Volume of a cylinder

$$\text{Volume of a cylinder } (V_c) = \pi \,(3.14) \times r^2$$
$$(\text{radius} \times \text{radius}) \times \text{height}$$
$$V_c = \pi \times r^2 \times h$$

QUESTION 1

What is the volume of a can that has a radius of 5 cm and a height of 14 cm?

Answer:

QUESTION 2

What is the volume of an ice cream tub that has a radius of 15 cm and a height of 90 cm?

Answer:

QUESTION 3

A double action pump has a radius of 14 cm and a height of 45 cm. What volume of air can be pumped?

Answer:

QUESTION 4

A large coffee can used in a coffee shop has a radius of 12 cm and a height of 28 cm. How much coffee can it hold?

Answer:

QUESTION 5

A large soup can has a radius of 13 cm and a height of 26 cm. What is its volume?

Answer:

QUESTION 6

A gas bottle used for cooking a barbeque has a radius of 17 cm and a height of 60 cm. How much gas could it hold?

Answer:

QUESTION 7

A large container of vegetable oil used in a restaurant is poured into 3 containers. Each container has a radius of 8 cm and a height of 20 cm.

a What is the volume of each container?

Answer:

b What is the volume of all 3 containers in total?

Answer:

QUESTION 8

A container used for pool chlorine has a radius of 10 cm and a height of 55 cm.

a What is its volume?

Answer:

b If half is used up during summer, how much is left?

Answer:

QUESTION 9

A water bottle has a radius of 8 cm and a height of 22 cm.

a What is its volume?

Answer:

_____

b If you use half during the day, how much is left?

Answer:

_____

QUESTION 10

A container for children's toys has a radius of 26 cm and a height of 80 cm. What is its volume?

Answer:

_____

Unit 11: Earning Wages

QUESTION 1

A shop assistant earns $98.50 clear per week for 10 hours work. How much does she earn per year, given that she works the same number of hours each week? (Note also that there are 52 weeks in a year.)

Answer:

QUESTION 2

A checkout assistant starts a shift at a department store at 10.00 a.m. and stops for a break at 1.30 p.m. He starts again at 2.00 p.m. then finishes the shift at 4.15 p.m.

a How many hours and minutes has he worked?

Answer:

b How much will he earn if he gets paid $8.20 per hour?

Answer:

QUESTION 3

QUESTION 4

Over a 6-day week, the takings for a coffee shop are: $465.80, $2,490.50, $556.20, $1,560.70 and $990.60. What are the total takings?

Answer:

A waitress earns $15.50 an hour and works a 38-hour week. How much are her gross earnings (before tax)?

Answer:

QUESTION 5

A short order cook needs the following amount of time to cook 5 orders: 14 minutes, 11 minutes, 7 minutes, 15 minutes and 9 minutes. How much time has been spent on cooking the orders? State your answer in hours and minutes.

Answer:

QUESTION 6

A department store café worker prepares food for lunch. The tasks take 4 ½ hours to complete. If the waitress gets $9.60 an hour, how much will she earn during this time?

Answer:

QUESTION 7

Over a shift a shop assistant spends 3 ½ hours stocking shelves and 2 ½ hours working on the front counter. If the shop assistant gets paid $11.80 per hour, how much does she earn during this shift?

Answer:

QUESTION 8

A banquet needs to be prepared in advance by the kitchen staff. They take 3.5 hours preparing the food for the banquet, 1.5 hours preparing and decorating the tables and 0.5 hours preparing drinks. How long in hours and minutes has all of the preparations taken?

Answer:

QUESTION 9

A cook starts work at 7.00 a.m. to prepare breakfast and works until 3.00 p.m. He has a morning break that lasts for 20 minutes, a lunch break for 60 minutes and an afternoon break of 20 minutes.

a How much time has he spent on breaks?

Answer:

b How much time has he spent working?

Answer:

QUESTION 10

The total cost of a bulk purchase of books for a bookstore is $2850.50. If it took 12 hours to prepare, load and deliver the books, how much is the rate per hour?

Answer:

9780170462792

Unit 12: Squaring Numbers

Section A: Introducing square numbers

Short-answer questions

Specific instructions to students

- This section is designed to help you to both improve your skills and to increase your speed in squaring numbers.
- Read the following questions and answer all of them in the spaces provided.
- You may not use a calculator.
- You need to show all working.

> **Any number squared is multiplied by itself.**

EXAMPLE

4 squared $= 4^2 = 4 \times 4 = 16$

QUESTION 1

$6^2 =$

Answer:

_____

QUESTION 2

$8^2 =$

Answer:

_____

QUESTION 3

$12^2 =$

Answer:

_____

QUESTION 4

$3^2 =$

Answer:

_____

QUESTION 5

$7^2 =$

Answer:

_____

QUESTION 6

$11^2 =$

Answer:

_____

QUESTION 7

$10^2 =$

Answer:

_____

QUESTION 8

$9^2 =$

Answer:

_____

QUESTION 9

$2^2 =$

Answer:

_____

QUESTION 10

$4^2 =$

Answer:

_____

QUESTION 11

$5^2 =$

Answer:

_____

Section B: Applying square numbers to the trade

QUESTION 1

The table area for a book display measures 2.8 m × 2.8 m. What area does it take up?

Answer:

QUESTION 2

The area for a display board measures 2.2 m × 2.2 m. What is the total area?

Answer:

QUESTION 3

The dimensions of a function room at a hotel are 12.6 m × 12.6 m. What is the total area?

Answer:

QUESTION 4

A shop manager has an area for setting up an audio visual display that is 3.5 m × 3.5 m. How much area is this?

Answer:

QUESTION 5

A store has floor area available for presentations of goods which measures 23 m × 23 m. If the checkout area measures 3 m × 3 m, how much area is left?

Answer:

QUESTION 6

An assistant store manager has a sheet of advertising board that is 2.4 m × 1.2 m. If 30 cm × 30 cm is cut out for pop-out displays, how much is left for other advertising?

Answer:

QUESTION 7

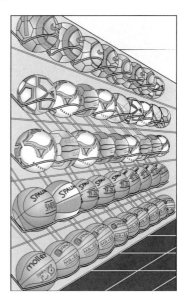

A sports store has a base area that measures 1.5 m × 1.5 m for a ball display. How much floor area does this take up?

Answer:

QUESTION 8

The base of a television advertising display measures 3.56 m × 3.56 m. What is the total area?

Answer:

_____

QUESTION 9

A mobile phone outlet has a floor area of 4.2 m × 4.2 m. What is the total area?

Answer:

_____

QUESTION 10

The walls of a major department store are to be decorated with advertising. The dimensions of the wall are 37 m × 37 m.

a What is the total wall area?

Answer:

_____

b If it costs $7.00 to paint one square metre, how much will it cost to paint 375 square metres?

Answer:

_____

Unit 13: Purchase Plans

Short-answer questions

Specific instructions to students

- This unit will help you to calculate the details of purchase plans.
- Read the following questions and answer all of them in the spaces provided.
- You may not use a calculator.
- You need to show all working.

There are many different options customers can choose from to pay for a purchase. Many stores offer a discounted 'hot price' for a product if you buy it on the spot, or you could pay for it over a certain time period, such as over four years. Alternatively, other stores offer the products for hire. But what is the difference in the final amount paid between the two payment options?

EXAMPLE

A 50″ full HD Plasma TV retails at $3191. The 4-year or 48-month plan means that the buyer pays $27.15 per week over 4 years.

$27.15 (per week)

    × 52 (52 weeks over 1 year)

    = $1411.80 (total over 1 year)

then

    × 4 (over 4 years)

    = $5647.20 (total paid)

Therefore:

4-year/48-month plan price: $5647.20

Retail price = $3191.00

Difference = $2456.20

Therefore, the difference is an extra $2456.20 that would be needed to be paid off over 4 years.

Solve the following questions.
(Note that 1 inch = 2.54 cm.)

QUESTION 1

A 52″ full HD LCD TV retails for $2997. The 4-year or 48-month payment plan means that the buyer pays $25.50 per week over 4 years. What is the price difference between the two payment options?

Answer:

QUESTION 2

A 42″ plasma TV retails for $898. The 4-year or 48-month payment plan means that the buyer pays $7.64 per week over 4 years. What is the price difference between the two payment options?

Answer:

QUESTION 3

A 60″ full HD plasma TV retails for $4997. The 4-year or 48-month payment plan means that the buyer pays $45.52 per week over 4 years. What is the price difference between the two payment options?

Answer:

QUESTION 4

A 42″ full HD LCD TV retails for $1596. The 4-year or 48-month payment plan means that the buyer pays $13.58 per week over 4 years. What is the price difference between the two payment options?

Answer:

9780170462792

QUESTION 5

A 58″ full HD plasma TV retails for $5998. The 4-year or 48-month payment plan means that the buyer pays $51.04 per week over 4 years. What is the price difference between the two payment options?

Answer:

QUESTION 6

A 52″ full HD LCD TV retails for $2997. The 4-year or 48-month payment plan means that the buyer pays $25.50 per week over 4 years. What is the price difference between the two payment options?

Answer:

QUESTION 7

A twin HD tuner with 200 GB HDD recorder retails for $898. The 4-year or 48-month payment plan means that the buyer pays $7.64 per week over 4 years. What is the price difference between the two payment options?

Answer:

QUESTION 8

A 15″ notebook laptop computer retails for $645. The store has a 'cashback' offer which means that the final cost will be $496. How much is the 'cashback' offer worth?

Answer:

QUESTION 9

A desktop computer retails for $1962. There is an option to rent/buy plan for $17.80 per week.

a How many weeks would it take until the retail price is reached?

Answer:

b If it was purchased over 36 months, how much more would you pay than if you bought it outright?

Answer:

QUESTION 10

A desktop computer retails for $1525. There is an option to rent/buy plan for $15.50 per week. If it was purchased over 36 months, how much more would you pay than if you bought it outright?

Answer:

Retail
Practice Written Exam
for the Retail Trade

Reading time: 10 minutes

Writing time: 1 hour 30 minutes

Section A: Literacy

Section B: General Mathematics

Section C: Trade Mathematics

QUESTION and ANSWER BOOK

Section	Topic	Number of questions	Marks
A	Literacy	7	22
B	General Mathematics	11	25
C	Trade Mathematics	40	53
		Total 58	Total 100

> The sections may be completed in the order of your choice.
> NO CALCULATORS are to be used during the exam.

Spelling

Read the passage below, and then underline the 20 spelling errors.

10 marks

Paula and Jean shopped at three diferent malls in the one day. It was the end of the financhial year and the sales were on. Over 115 shops had sales on and the shoping hours had been extunded. Normaly, the malls would open at 8.00 a.m. and closed at 5.00 p.m., however, with the ecstended hours, all malls were oppen untill 9.00 p.m. everyday. Everyone was excited. Retale thurapy was at hand!

The jewelery stores had plenty to sell with necklaces being one of the most poplar choices. The book stores also had a huge runge of stock on sale, as did the health food stores. The mall was buzing with people and the food courts were very popular. Paula and Jean found the perfame sales to their liking the most, and they shoped around for different fragrances for hours. With their arms full, they headed off at just after clossing time. They had really enjoyyed their gractc day out shopping, but they both felt that they could now do with a good long breake!

Correct the spelling errors by writing them out with the correct spelling below.

_____

_____

Alphabetising

Put the following words into alphabetical order.

6 marks

Entrance	Stainless steel
Customer	Bedding
Service	Credit
Compact disk	Rewards
Clothing	Designer names
Homeware	Mattress
Assistant manager	Kitchen goods

_____

_____

_____

_____

_____

_____

Comprehension

Short answer questions

Specific instructions to students

- Read the following activity and then answer the questions accordingly.

Read the following passage and answer the questions on the following page.

Brad started work at the local shopping centre on a Thursday night. He knew it would be busy because Thursday night was always popular for families, students and couples who all enjoyed shopping at the centre. Brad's tasks included cleaning the floors, stocking the shelves and working at the checkout. Although Brad was nervous, he soon was kept busy by all of the customers asking for help. The first customer he met approached him and asked: 'Do you have the newest computer game that came out on Monday?' Brad replied 'We do. It's in aisle 6 and there should still be plenty of them.' The customer headed off to purchase the game.

Brad was starting to enjoy his new job when a second customer came to him and inquired, 'You got DVD players?'

Brad thought for a moment. 'Yeah,' Brad then replied, 'they're in the audiovisual section'

'Well don't just stand there,' the rude young man demanded, 'show me where they are. You've got nothing better to do!'

Brad said nothing, but instead showed the young man the aisle and left him there to look at the products. There was a big contrast between the first and second customer, and Brad was not as happy as he was moments ago. As the night wore on, he soon realised that although most customers were kind and had good manners, others could be very rude. He had learned a lot on his first shift.

QUESTION 1   1 mark

Why were Thursday nights busy at the shopping centre?

Answer:

_____

_____

QUESTION 2   1 mark

What did Brad's tasks involve?

Answer:

_____

_____

QUESTION 3   1 mark

What was the first customer keen to purchase?

Answer:

_____

_____

QUESTION 4   1 mark

What was the second customer keen to purchase?

Answer:

_____

_____

QUESTION 5   2 marks

What did Brad learn about customers on his first night?

Answer:

_____

_____

Section B: General Mathematics

QUESTION 1   1 + 1 + 1 = 3 marks

What unit of measurement would you use to measure:

a the length of a display table?

Answer:

_____

b the store temperature?

Answer:

_____

c cleaning fluid?

Answer:

_____

QUESTION 2   1 + 1 + 1 = 3 marks

Write an example of the following and give an instance of where it may be found in the retail industry:

a percentages?

Answer:

_____

b decimals?

Answer:

_____

c fractions?

Answer:

_____

QUESTION 3   1 + 1 = 2 marks

Convert the following units:

a 8 kilograms to grams

Answer:

_____

b 1500 g to kg

Answer:

_____

QUESTION 4   1 mark

Write the following in descending order:

0.7   0.71   7.1   70.1   701.00   7.0

Answer:

_____

QUESTION 5   1 + 1 = 2 marks

Write the decimal number that is between the following:

a 0.1 and 0.2

Answer:

_____

b 1.3 and 1.4

Answer:

_____

QUESTION 6   1 + 1 = 2 marks

Round off the following numbers to two (2) decimal places:

a 5.177

Answer:

_____

b 12.655

Answer:

_____

QUESTION 7   1 + 1 = 2 marks

Estimate the following by approximation:

a 101×81

Answer:

_____

b 399×21

Answer:

_____

QUESTION 8   1 + 1 = 2 marks

What do the following add up to?

a $7, $13.57 and $163.99

Answer:

_____

b 4, 5.73 and 229.57

Answer:

_____

QUESTION 9   1 + 1 = 2 marks

Subtract the following:

a 196 from 813

Answer:

_____

b 5556 from 9223

Answer:

_____

QUESTION 10   1 + 1 = 2 marks

Use division to solve:

a $4824 \div 3$

Answer:

_____

b $84.2 \div 0.4$

Answer:

_____

QUESTION 11   2 + 2 = 4 marks

Using BODMAS solve:

a $(3 \times 7) \times 4 + 9 - 5$

Answer:

_____

b $(8 \times 12) \times 2 + 8 - 4$

Answer:

_____

Section C: Trade Mathematics

Basic operations

Addition

QUESTION 1   1 mark

A shopper purchases 500 g of roast beef, 350 g of sliced chicken loaf and 150 g of ham. How many grams of food is that in total?

Answer:

_____

QUESTION 2   1 mark

A shopper buys the following vegetables: 2 kg of tomatoes, 3 kg of onions and 10 kg of potatoes. How many kg of food has been purchased in total?

Answer:

_____

Subtraction

QUESTION 1   1 mark

A surf and ski shop sells 57 bracelets from a box that contains 150 bracelets. How many bracelets remain in the box?

Answer:

_____

QUESTION 2   1 mark

A shopper's skate gear purchase comes to $344. At the cash register, the store manager discounts the purchase by $35 as the shop is having a sale on all of its skate gear. How much does the bill total now?

Answer:

_____

Multiplication

QUESTION 1   1 mark

A supermarket shopper buys 4 lettuces for $3 each, 2 onions for 35 cents each and 2 avocados costing $1 each. What is the total cost?

Answer:

_____

QUESTION 2   1 mark

Bread rolls are purchased for a dinner party. If one bread roll costs 25 cents, how much will 25 bread rolls cost?

Answer:

_____

Division

QUESTION 1   1 mark

An interstate semi-trailer travels 1125 km over a 5-day haul delivering clothing to country retail outlets. Approximately how many kilometres are covered, on average, each day?

Answer:

_____

_____

QUESTION 2   1 mark

At a yearly stocktake, a storeperson counts 720 of the same toys. If there needs to be 12 toys in each box, how many boxes are there?

Answer:

_____

Decimals

Addition

QUESTION 1   1 mark

A family buys the following from a pet store: a dog kennel for $199.95, a water bowl $19.50 and a 5 kg bag of dry pet food for $34.50. How much do the purchases cost in total?

Answer:

_____

QUESTION 2   1 mark

A shopper has several lay-by orders that are to be collected before Christmas. One totals $139.80, another is $430.65 and the last adds up to $216.45. How much is the total for all three?

Answer:

_____

9780170462792

Subtraction

QUESTION 1   1 mark

A shop assistant works 38 hours and earns $418.50. She then spends $55 on petrol and a further $25 on a mobile phone recharge card. How much is left?

Answer:

_____

QUESTION 2   1 mark

A stainless steel cooking set is purchased for a cost of $148.50. If it is paid for with two $100 notes, how much change will be given?

Answer:

_____

Multiplication

QUESTION 1   1 + 1 = 2 marks

A shopper goes to a music store where DVDs are on sale for $19.95 each. The shopper buys 6.

a How much do the 6 DVDs total?

Answer:

_____

b How much change will be needed from $150.00?

Answer:

_____

QUESTION 2   1 + 1 = 2 marks

A café worker purchases 9 cartons of soft drink at a cost of $14.50 each.

a How much do the 9 cartons of soft drink cost in total?

Answer:

_____

b How much change will be received from $150.00?

Answer:

_____

Division

QUESTION 1   1 mark

An electronics shop takes in $4455.00 over 8 hours during their Lightning Sale. How much does this work out to on average, per hour?

Answer:

_____

QUESTION 2   1 mark

A group of 4 people order food from a menu from a restaurant. The bill comes to $48.60. How much is the bill for each person if they divide it equally?

Answer:

_____

Fractions

QUESTION 1   1 mark

$\frac{2}{3} + \frac{3}{4} = ?$

Answer:

_____

QUESTION 2   1 mark

$\frac{4}{5} - \frac{1}{3} = ?$

Answer:

_____

QUESTION 3   1 mark

$\frac{2}{3} \times \frac{1}{4} = ?$

Answer:

_____

QUESTION 4   1 mark

$\frac{3}{4} \div \frac{1}{2} = ?$

Answer:

_____

Percentages

QUESTION 1   1 + 1 = **2 marks**

A shop assistant in a hardware store marks down circular saws by 10%. Each circular saw costs $249.00 and there is a 10% off sale.

a How much is the discount worth?

Answer:

_____

b What is the price of each saw after the discount?

Answer:

_____

QUESTION 2   1 + 1 + 1 = **3 marks**

Shoes are discounted by 20%. The regular retail price of a certain pair is $120.00 each.

a How much is the discount worth?

Answer:

_____

b What is the price of the shoes after the discount?

Answer:

_____

c How much change would be needed if a $100.00 was used to pay for one pair of the shoes?

Answer:

_____

Measurement

QUESTION 1   1 **mark**

How many grams are there in 3.85 kg?

Answer:

_____

QUESTION 2   1 **mark**

2285 millimetres converts to how many metres?

Answer:

_____

Circumference

QUESTION 1   1 **mark**

What is the circumference of a display table with a diameter of 100 cm?

Answer:

_____

QUESTION 2   1 **mark**

What is the circumference of a flood light with a diameter of 28 cm?

Answer:

_____

Diameter

QUESTION 1   1 **mark**

What is the diameter of a round mirror with a circumference of 314 cm?

Answer:

_____

QUESTION 2   1 **mark**

What is the diameter of a round table top with a circumference of 157 cm?

Answer:

_____

Area

QUESTION 1   1 **mark**

An area set aside to display toys measures 15 m by 12 m. What is the total floor area?

Answer:

_____

QUESTION 2   1 **mark**

What is the total floor area of an outdoor furniture display that measures 11 m by 10 m?

Answer:

_____

Volume of a cube

QUESTION 1   1 mark

A cold room at a patisserie measures 6 m long by 3 m wide by 2 m high. How many cubic metres of space is there?

Answer:

_____

QUESTION 2   1 mark

A storage box used by a retail store is 80 cm long, 30 cm wide and 45 cm tall. How many cubic centimetres are available for storage?

Answer:

_____

Volume of a cylinder

QUESTION 1   2 marks

A large storage drum for toys has a radius of 15 cm and a height of 45 cm. What is its total volume?

Answer:

_____

QUESTION 2   2 marks

A biscuit tin has a radius of 10 cm and a height of 25 cm. What is its volume?

Answer:

_____

Earning wages

QUESTION 1   2 marks

A checkout person gets paid $9.50 per hour. If he works 15 hours a week, how much will his gross pay be?

Answer:

_____

QUESTION 2   2 marks

A waiter prepares food for lunch. The tasks take 2 ½ hours to complete. If the waiter gets paid $12.60 an hour, how much will be earned for this time?

Answer:

_____

Squaring numbers

QUESTION 1   2 marks

What is 7^2?

Answer:

_____

QUESTION 2   2 marks

The floor area of an electronics shop measures 13×13 metres. What is the total area?

Answer:

_____

Purchase plans

QUESTION 1   2 marks

A 42″ plasma TV retails for $1235. The 4-year or 48-month payment plan means that the buyer pays $8.64 per week over 4 years or 48 months. What is the price difference between buying with cash and purchasing using hire purchase?

Answer:

_____

QUESTION 2   2 marks

A 15″ notebook laptop computer retails for $963. The store has a 'cashback' offer which means that the final cost will be $689. How much is the 'cashback' offer worth?

Answer:

_____

Formulae and Data

Circumference of a Circle

$C = \pi \times d$
where: C = circumference, π = 3.14, d = diameter

Diameter of a Circle

Diameter (d) of a circle = $\dfrac{\text{circumference}}{\pi\ (3.14)}$

Area

Area = length $\times$ breadth and is given in square units
$\quad$ = $l \times b$

Volume of a Cube

Volume = length $\times$ width $\times$ height and is given in cubic units
$\quad$ = $l \times w \times h$

Volume of a Cylinder

Volume of a cylinder (V_c) = $\pi\ (3.14) \times r^2$ (radius $\times$ radius) $\times$ height
$$V_c = \pi \times r^2 \times h$$

9780170462792

Times Tables

1

1 × 1	=	1
2 × 1	=	2
3 × 1	=	3
4 × 1	=	4
5 × 1	=	5
6 × 1	=	6
7 × 1	=	7
8 × 1	=	8
9 × 1	=	9
10 × 1	=	10
11 × 1	=	11
12 × 1	=	12

2

1 × 2	=	2
2 × 2	=	4
3 × 2	=	6
4 × 2	=	8
5 × 2	=	10
6 × 2	=	12
7 × 2	=	14
8 × 2	=	16
9 × 2	=	18
10 × 2	=	20
11 × 2	=	22
12 × 2	=	24

3

1 × 3	=	3
2 × 3	=	6
3 × 3	=	9
4 × 3	=	12
5 × 3	=	15
6 × 3	=	18
7 × 3	=	21
8 × 3	=	24
9 × 3	=	27
10 × 3	=	30
11 × 3	=	33
12 × 3	=	36

4

1 × 4	=	4
2 × 4	=	8
3 × 4	=	12
4 × 4	=	16
5 × 4	=	20
6 × 4	=	24
7 × 4	=	28
8 × 4	=	32
9 × 4	=	36
10 × 4	=	40
11 × 4	=	44
12 × 4	=	48

5

1 × 5	=	5
2 × 5	=	10
3 × 5	=	15
4 × 5	=	20
5 × 5	=	25
6 × 5	=	30
7 × 5	=	35
8 × 5	=	40
9 × 5	=	45
10 × 5	=	50
11 × 5	=	55
12 × 5	=	60

6

1 × 6	=	6
2 × 6	=	12
3 × 6	=	18
4 × 6	=	24
5 × 6	=	30
6 × 6	=	36
7 × 6	=	42
8 × 6	=	48
9 × 6	=	54
10 × 6	=	60
11 × 6	=	66
12 × 6	=	72

7

1 × 7	=	7
2 × 7	=	14
3 × 7	=	21
4 × 7	=	28
5 × 7	=	35
6 × 7	=	42
7 × 7	=	49
8 × 7	=	56
9 × 7	=	63
10 × 7	=	70
11 × 7	=	77
12 × 7	=	84

8

1 × 8	=	8
2 × 8	=	16
3 × 8	=	24
4 × 8	=	32
5 × 8	=	40
6 × 8	=	48
7 × 8	=	56
8 × 8	=	64
9 × 8	=	72
10 × 8	=	80
11 × 8	=	88
12 × 8	=	96

9

1 × 9	=	9
2 × 9	=	18
3 × 9	=	27
4 × 9	=	36
5 × 9	=	45
6 × 9	=	54
7 × 9	=	63
8 × 9	=	72
9 × 9	=	81
10 × 9	=	90
11 × 9	=	99
12 × 9	=	108

10

1 × 10	=	10
2 × 10	=	20
3 × 10	=	30
4 × 10	=	40
5 × 10	=	50
6 × 10	=	60
7 × 10	=	70
8 × 10	=	80
9 × 10	=	90
10 × 10	=	100
11 × 10	=	110
12 × 10	=	120

11

1 × 11	=	11
2 × 11	=	22
3 × 11	=	33
4 × 11	=	44
5 × 11	=	55
6 × 11	=	66
7 × 11	=	77
8 × 11	=	88
9 × 11	=	99
10 × 11	=	110
11 × 11	=	121
12 × 11	=	132

12

1 × 12	=	12
2 × 12	=	24
3 × 12	=	36
4 × 12	=	48
5 × 12	=	60
6 × 12	=	72
7 × 12	=	84
8 × 12	=	96
9 × 12	=	108
10 × 12	=	120
11 × 12	=	132
12 × 12	=	144

Multiplication Grid

	1	2	3	4	5	6	7	8	9	10	11	12
1	1	2	3	4	5	6	7	8	9	10	11	12
2	2	4	6	8	10	12	14	16	18	20	22	24
3	3	6	9	12	15	18	21	24	27	30	33	36
4	4	8	12	16	20	24	28	32	36	40	44	48
5	5	10	15	20	25	30	35	40	45	50	55	60
6	6	12	18	24	30	36	42	48	54	60	66	72
7	7	14	21	28	35	42	49	56	63	70	77	84
8	8	16	24	32	40	48	56	64	72	80	88	96
9	9	18	27	36	45	54	63	72	81	90	99	108
10	10	20	30	40	50	60	70	80	90	100	110	120
11	11	22	33	44	55	66	77	88	99	110	121	132
12	12	24	36	48	60	72	84	96	108	120	132	144

9780170462792

Notes

Notes

Notes

Notes

Notes

Notes